AFTER THE STORM

A book of poems depicting the journey of an abuse survivor

By

Janet Bale

After The Storm
A book of poems depicting the journey of an abuse survivor.

First Edition

Copyright
© 2007 Janet Bale
All Rights Reserved

isbn: 978-1-84753-558-0

All profits from the sale of this book are being donated to

Registered charity 1088469

Contents

A Special Dedication	1
Ashamed	3
All Lies *	4
Who Am I?	6
Grannies Wardrobe	8
The Blanket Game	9
Little Sis	10
A Real Movie	11
The "Me" Inside	13
Shadows	15
Screaming	16
Abuse	17
Friendship	18
Betrayed Them All	20
Blame Me	21
Murderous Feelings Of Hate	23
Rape	24
Shadows Of The Past	25
Incest	26
You Know	27
The Cult Killed Her Babies	28
Unreachable	31
It's Over	33
Asking For Help	34
So Empty	35
Break The Chain	37
Standing By	38

Just Hanging In	39
My Precious Boy	40
I Envy You	41

The Later Years

Recovering From Depression	44
The Well	46
Abandoned	48
Numb	49
Moving On	51
Silent Scars *	52
I Ate Today	53
Morning	54
Winter Returns	55
The Visit	57
Just Thoughts *	58
You Matter!	59
Dwelling	61
Pull Myself Out	62
Keep Fighting *	64
Hold onto Me	65
Let It Be *	66
Resolve	67
After The Storm	69
Tripped Up	70
Squeeze My Heart	71
Flower	72

Show You Care	73
Please Yet Again?	74
Riding the Waves	76
Snow Drop	78
I Claim My Life	79
Where to?	80
Take Flight	81
Bubbles	82
Friends	83

Please note: poems should be read with caution, as several could trigger an unwanted reaction by someone in a delicate emotional state.

Some of the poems (flagged with an *) and all the illustrations are reproduced with the kind permission of others who have shared similar childhood abuse experiences.

ACKNOWLEDGEMENTS

I would like to thank

My friends – your thanks are scattered throughout the book!

My children, who won't ever know that I've written this. They don't have to as I've broken the chain; but I do want to acknowledge the strength that I've gained from their love.

Lonely for her illustrations, poems and continuing encouragement

MoJo, Shanothan and *Sumday* for their contributions,

& *Peggy* for allowing me to tell her story.

Also *you*, for purchasing this book.

Maybe you have done so hoping that it might help you discover you're not alone or you want to try and understand so you can help others.

Whatever your reason, you're already helping me to create some good out of what happened, since profits from the sale of this book are going to support the work of EVA – Emerging from Violence & Abuse
(Registered charity 1088469)

A Special Dedication

You are a really special person
I am honoured to call you a friend

I want to thank you for your patience
For listening
And Encouragement

For being there for me
As I struggled to come to terms
With my past
Fighting off depression
And at the many crossroads that have come along

Thank you for sharing some of the journey with me

You really are a special person
I am privileged to have you as a friend

Ashamed

Ashamed of what I am
Afraid of my past
What will people say
If they knew
How terrible I am?

I need their friendship
But I've been so bad
Keep trying to make up for it
As if I could

I don't deserve this life
Yet somehow I'm still here

I wish I didn't hurt so much
I wish it was all over

But somehow I must keep going on
Try to make up for what I've done
Not that I'll ever succeed
But one day this torment will end
And I'll be allowed to rest
In the deep dark depths
OF NOTHINGNESS

All Lies

But we know the truth
They do too
But they close their eyes, try not to look

All lies

Pretending it didn't happen
That life is all sweet and fair
Not looking; therefore not seeing

All lies

So how do we move on from this?
Shout out the truth
Don't Hide It

All lies

A different life lies ahead
A chance to make it better
Don't hide their lies

All lies

Others pretend they do not know
They're trying to keep you quiet
Just like the hand across your mouth

All lies

They're so desperate to hurt you
To keep the truth inside
Away from the gazing look of others

All lies

Admit the truth
Don't defend their lies,
The blame is not yours to take

All lies

And as you make the truth unfold
You begin your healing journey
You will survive, despite their lies

All lies

By Lonely & Snow Drop

WHO AM I?

A little about me,
Who am I?
Well to look at
I'm like any other woman
That you'd find in an office
Or walking around Tescos, with a trolley
I live in a 3 bed semi
I'm no different from anyone
Not on the outside

Inside I have a secret
Untold for nearly 20 years
It tears me apart
And has tried to ruin my life
Even now, I can't write down what it is.
As if putting it down in ink
A final admittance of what I've done, and what I am

The words you read, within this book
Are the inner side of me
So deep and hidden
Hidden from myself
Such that my mind wouldn't let me remember
Till struck down, then the truth came out.

What you read here
Is how I felt
As a child and then the woman I became
Not all you see happened to me
Others who have shared their pain
As I shared mine with them.
Some of what they said
The pictures that formed in my mind

As I heard their stories.
What happened to those friends and me
How I felt, trying to come to terms
So I could then rebuild my life.

Please as you read these words
Do not pity us.
Instead please do what you can
To help the "little ones"
Who are facing the evil
That I once faced
Help protect them
Help ease their suffering
Help make our world
A happier and safer place.

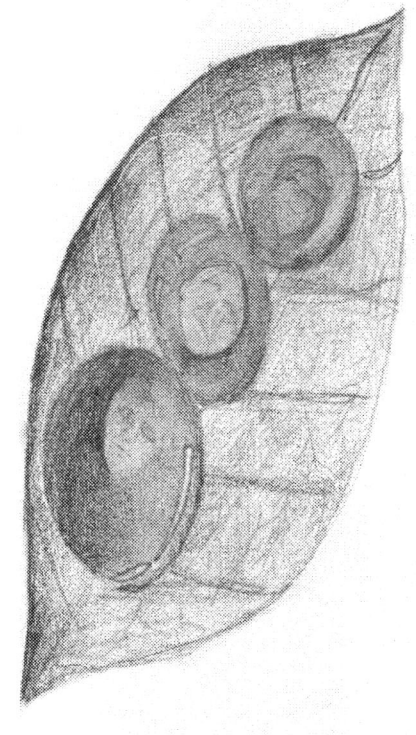

GRANNIES WARDROBE

Trying not to breathe
Mustn't make a sound
Grannies wardrobe smells of moth balls
But here I must stay
Here, is safe
He hasn't found me here before
He forgets how small I am

Eventually, he is gone
Again, I can breathe
This time I've made it
No ordeal today

The Blanket Game

The blanket game
That's what he called it
One of us would be a blanket
Resting on the other
Usually me below
Trapped by his weight
His strength
And the love I had for him.

Love?
Are you surprised?
Yes I love him
How could I not
At least he was there.
I don't like what he made me do
It hurt, and scared
But I am his
So must do as I'm told

The Blanket game
So I don't get cold.

Little Sis

He asked for me
A sister he wanted
Little did they know why

So I was his
To do as he pleased
And as he pleased
He did

They didn't ever realise
Couldn't see what they had done
Left him in charge
So I did what I was told!

They weren't there for him
They weren't there for me
Consumed in their own worlds
We were but accessories
Of the 'perfect looking' family

Little could those who looked on see
For all was hidden from view
Secrets
No don't say a word

They wouldn't believe
Anyway!

A Real Movie

It's like remembering a movie, you once saw
Only it's not, you know it's real
Looking on from the outside
The ultimate lie to yourself

Even now, I remember the tiles on the wall
The fluffy bathroom carpet
Soft on my back
Held down, not to make a noise

A secret game
Just between the two of us
Only this game isn't fun
But still it carries on

I don't understand
Is something wrong with me?
This game should be nice
Yet it hurts me.

Soon it'll be over
To my room I'll be able to retreat
Hide my pain and sorrow, from the world
At least until the next time.

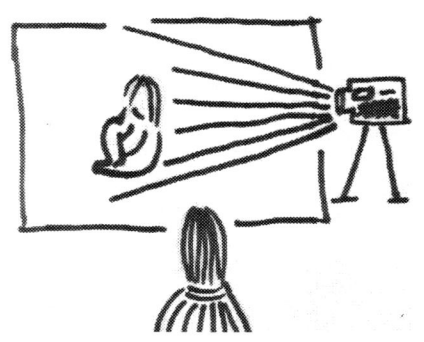

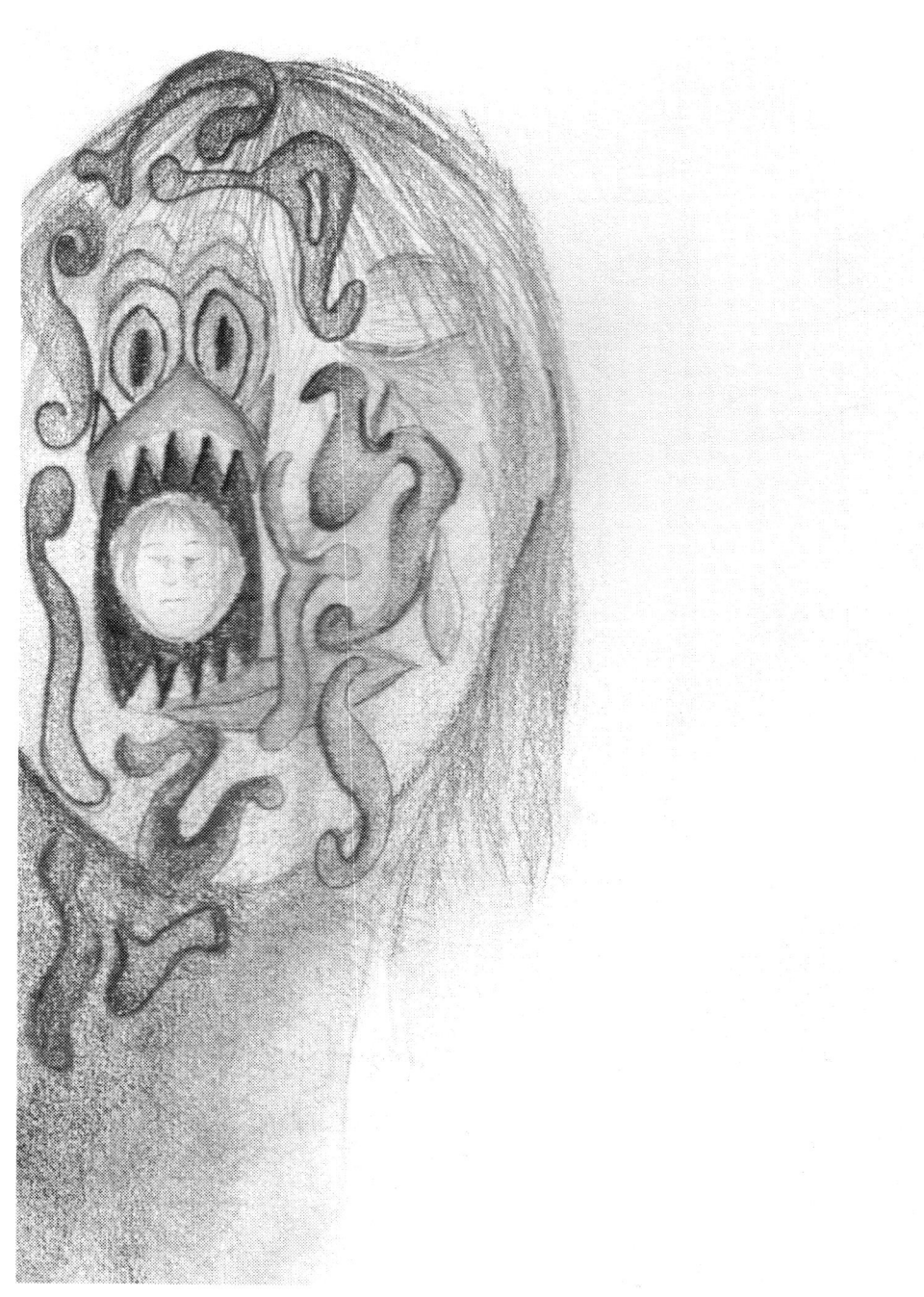

The "Me" Inside

The life I lead
Is a great big lie.
People don't know
The "me" inside.

They see a woman
Single minded
Looking after a home
A career, a son.

Confident, friendly
Who likes to have fun.

Nobody sees me.
I can't let them in.
The pain, no I can't risk that.
It's difficult for them
What they see on the outside
Is not who I am.

Maybe as the years have gone by
I've begun to believe the lie, too
But inside, hiding from the world.
Is a very frightened little girl.

Shadows

Shadows of the Past
Keep creeping up behind me
When will they strike next?
I can not tell

They haunt me
They follow me
No matter what I do
They still keep coming
No place to hide
To retreat
They're going to get me
SOON

I resist what they want
But still they keep on coming
I'm growing weary of the fight
I want to give in
Give up
But that would mean they've won

So tired I am now
Battle worn

I wish I could just curl up
And sink
To the deep dark depths
Of Death.

SCREAMING

Something, deep inside of me
Is screaming to get out.
Emotions well up
They can not be trapped.
If you trap them, they go sour and turn to poison.

Life is for living,
Moment by precious moment.
Time slips by so quickly
Happiness can be lost so easily

The sadness must be let out.
Painful though it will be,
To live as I've lived,
Hiding all emotion
For the fear, that I might get hurt.
Is not a life at all.

I fear what is to come
For so many years I've kept the secret
Now the time is here
I'm scared
But if I'm to have a life
Then this must be done.

Abuse

What is it?
Removal of rights that I never had.
Causing pain? Taking liberties?

I know what happened to me
Though sometimes it feels like a film I once saw
Or a fiendish nightmare.
Was it really me?
Sometimes I doubt myself
Though I know,
I'd rather pretend it was someone else.

I'm so screwed up now
I can't escape the truth
Though it makes me hate myself
I'd rather die, than face those nightmares
Face them I must
For over 20 years I've hidden them away
Hid from the truth
Now is the time to reopen those wounds
Get out the poison that's been haunting my life

Then let it heal.
There will always be a scar
How could there not?
From pain so deep I hid it from myself.

So now is the time
I fear this so much
What else will I remember?
What are the other horrors?

Buried deep inside my head

FRIENDSHIP

The hardest thing for me to do is reveal
                    who I am to other people.
Maybe I'm just scared, to be judged by those others,
To trust others

I ask myself, have I really been hurt that much?
Surely I would understand if a friend needed me
Yet to ask for help
To risk their refusal or worse still,
                        them not to understand.

Friendship, I hold so dear
A friend to me is a special sort of love.
Love, most people learn from their families
As they grow, parents who cared for the baby,
Care for the child, and always love.
Or so society would like us to believe.

I wish I could tell you that society is right.
But no. Not all children know that sort of love

Worse still it's the child who feels to blame.
What's so bad about me, that I couldn't be loved?
I will never know.

But as an adult now
My friends have shown me
The sort of kindness, caring
That I longed for as a child.

The pain of all those years
Not gone, but a future?

Knowing that maybe I matter - just a bit
That I am capable of love
And can be loved.

You, my friends
You've shown me
That the child no one noticed
Can still matter

And, as I wipe away the tear, that formed,
                    while thinking of you.
I wipe away the sadness of that little girl.
Now grown
Like a dying plant
Replanted, nurtured, fed and cared for
Starting to flower
To bring its own uniqueness
To the eyes of the world.

BETRAYED THEM ALL

All I ever wanted was their love
Never will that happen
I find I've learned to hate
Oh, how low can I go?
Become like them
Selfish
No not I!
I don't want to be like them
I'd rather die.

Family loyalty
I should never have told
But words said
Can not be undone
Now it's known
All of my shame
Yet the torture still continues
The pain will not subside
What I've done
Will never change
What I am, Have been
Remains the same.

How to make sense of this
I feel, I caused all this
Friends say it's not my fault
But I still can't believe that.

BLAME ME

The world around me
Laughing, Joyful
I see the humour
Raise a smile to be polite
Mustn't let them know
What thoughts are in my mind

I wonder what they really think
Blame me, I let it happen
They say it's not my fault
But I was there

The pain of those years
Still with me now
The sadness of the child
Who didn't know who to cry to.

The only one who cared
They tell me caused this pain

It wasn't his fault
He didn't mean to hurt me

Now I'm left, all confused
Can't work it out
All the things I've believed over the years
Thrown up in the air
Now scattered all around.

MURDEROUS FEELINGS OF HATE

Do you know what it's like to feel anger?
So strong, you'd wish you were dead?
Murderous feelings of hate
Betrayal, sadness and pain

I know those feelings all too well
So ashamed for feeling that way
I don't want to cause any more pain.
But when will the suffering end?

They hurt me
Hurt me bad
And I hate them
For not caring
Even now, years on
They don't know who I am
Never bothered to find out
Imagine me, the way they wanted me
Angry with me for not being who they want

And still they push their way into my life
Won't leave me alone
I've a new family now, all of my own
To love me, as I am.

The past should be buried
But in my mind
It will always live on.

Rape

Does that word send a chill down your spine?
It does mine.

Do you feel sick, when you hear of it?
I do.

I wonder what "normal" people feel.
Is it just me, who shivers inside?
Because, I truly know how it feels.
To be robbed so intimately
To feel like trash, or some sort of whore.

I don't mean to shock you
Nor to offend.
Questions are burning deep inside me,
I'm looking for answers.
That I guess I'll never find.

I wish that I could feel,
Like "normal" people feel.
I never can, of course
None of us can change who we are.
What we are, nor what we've done.
But maybe, eventually, peace may come.

SHADOWS OF THE PAST

Little me is very scared
Little me is hiding
Little me can feel them there
The shadows, just watching

Memories so vivid
So clear, yet some they blur
The pain, still with me
Duller, but constant

They're watching over me
But impotent to help
One day they'll be able to
But for now, no one to turn to

So little me just carries on
Pretends it isn't happening
Tries to live in an imaginary world
Where all the love is

Dreams of far off places
Where others really care
Someone to protect little me
Oh how I wish that I were there

Why does no one notice?
Why can they not see?
Only the shadows watching over know
The pain of little me

INCEST

I need you to understand
But you're blinded by a word
Society says something is wrong
So guilt follows
But it wasn't all bad
It just wasn't like that
You see I loved him
And he I
An inappropriate love

Yes
Wrong?
I think not

The blame is not his
Nor is it mine
We were children
Mixed up in a strange world of lies
Comfort we sought
And comfort we found

I still love him now
Though scars of long ago still show
The scars are not from what we did
But the love, that we weren't shown

He hurts now, as much as I
I want to help him
But know not how
I need your strength
But understanding more
Please try to see
Beyond that word

You Know

Now you know
Do you think of me any differently?
Now I've let you in

Do you think I'm weak?
It was all my fault
That's what I think, you'll think

I disgust myself
For who I am
How can I expect you to feel another way?

But maybe if you do
Then maybe I can believe, what others have said
That it wasn't me, it was him

Maybe I can extend myself
The understanding, that I so need from you
Maybe, one day, even accept myself

So tell me that you understand
I need your reassurance
To help me on the mend

THE CULT KILLED HER BABIES

I just had to write this down
Round and round my head it goes
Since she told me what they did

Lost her mother at five
Father f**ked her up
Then let his mates
Do just the same
She didn't deserve that!

How did they manage
To do such stuff
Unnoticed?
Home schooled was little Peggy
Nobody there for her

At Christmas time Santa had a go
But Halloween was worse
One day when she tried to fight
Her father threw
Her teddy on the fire

At 12 she had her first child
They killed it right in front of her
Six hours old
Sacrificed to the Devil

Then another baby
She thought she might keep that
But six days old they killed this too
Sacrificed to the Devil

The final came and lived six weeks
Sacrificed again
Lucifer's Child they branded her
In a barren upside down upon her foot

At 15 she was rescued
To a foster home she went
Now a few years later
She's tried to kill herself again

Other men still rape and abuse her
Men she should be able to trust
They call her whore, and slut and worse
No wonder she hates herself

She won't eat
Doesn't like food within her mouth
They did that to her
Through their torment and their wrath

She's 18 now
And oh so damaged
Can't see a future
Can't protect herself
Never been taught
The little girl
So all alone
Abused
Now doing their abusing for them

This is a true story, horrific as it is.
Thank you Peggy for letting me disclose it.

Unreachable

Slipping
Sliding
Tumbling
Down

Reaching
Grabbing
Nothing
To hold

Screaming
Shouting
Listening
No sound

Except
Echoing
My thoughts
Howling

Alone
No help
No fight left

CRYING FORLORN

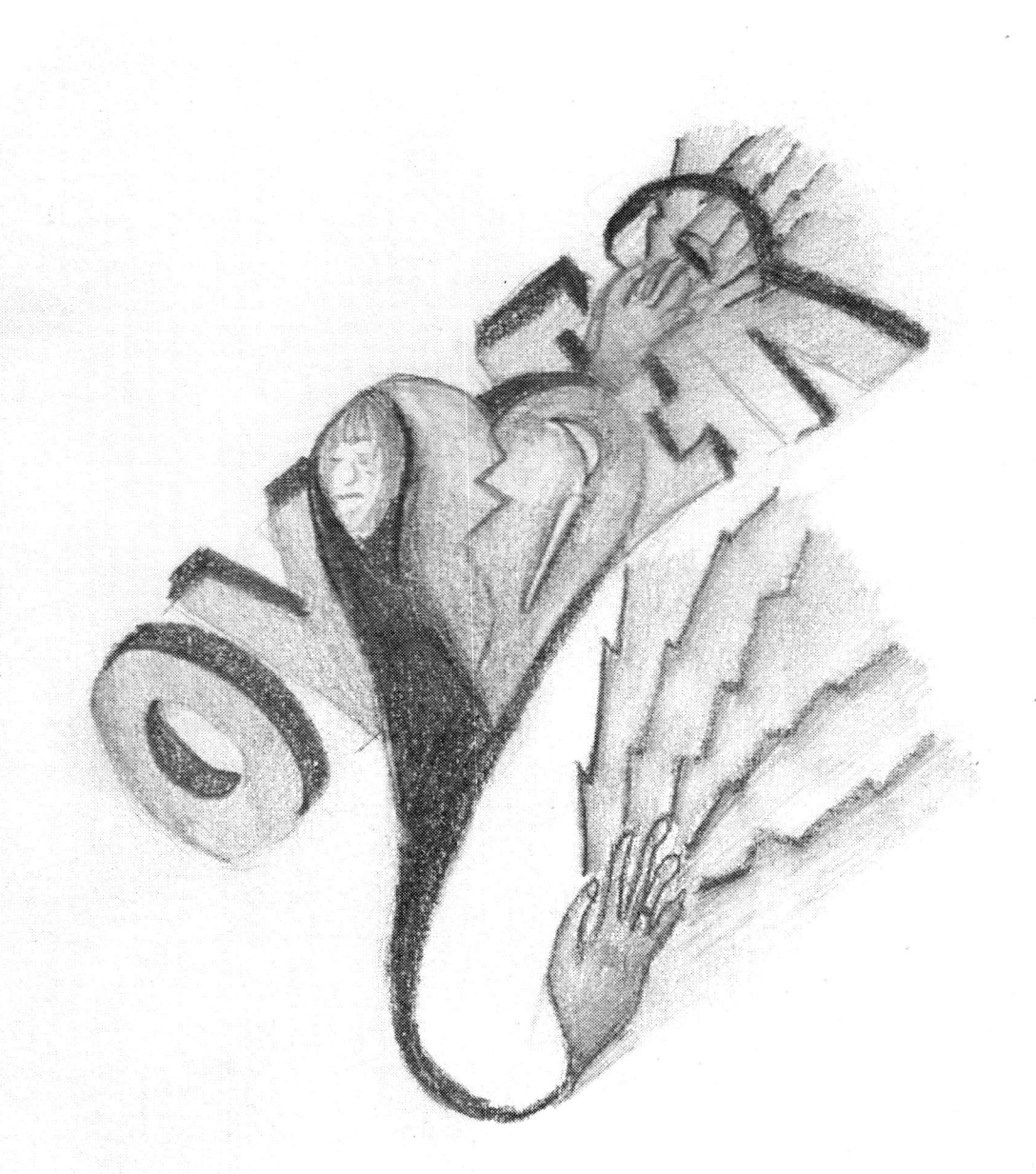

It's Over

Darkness all around
Silence, quiet and peaceful.
An owl hoots, the only soul awake
To keep me company

Darkness fills my heart
Sink down, dwell in fear
Somewhere a hand stretched out
I can't grab hold, I can't GRAB HOLD

Darkness is swallowing me
I'm falling, falling
I've gone too far, I can't get up.
It's over, OVER.

ASKING FOR HELP

Asking for help
Is the hardest thing
I keep crying out
But no sound is coming

I'm scared, that I'll be too much
That you'll grow, tired of me

My need is constant
There's no relief
I just really need you
To simply, hold onto me

Hold me till it flows away
Hold me till its' gone
Tell me that'll be OK
Tell me when I'm safe

The nightmares keep coming back
I know you don't understand
You weren't there, you couldn't know
And I don't explain very well

I don't want to tire you
I don't want to bore you
I really need your support
I understand this is not your fight

But on my own
I'm scared

I'LL ABORT.

So Empty

I look around me
I feel such pain
Not physical
But such a deep loneliness
So empty
Oh how I wish I could feel love
To show you how much I care

I don't know how to feel it
To be wanted, needed

With friends I feel like I'm imposing
They don't need a weight like me

And now in writing this
A tear drips down my cheek
I think maybe it's the first time in years
That I've cried for me.

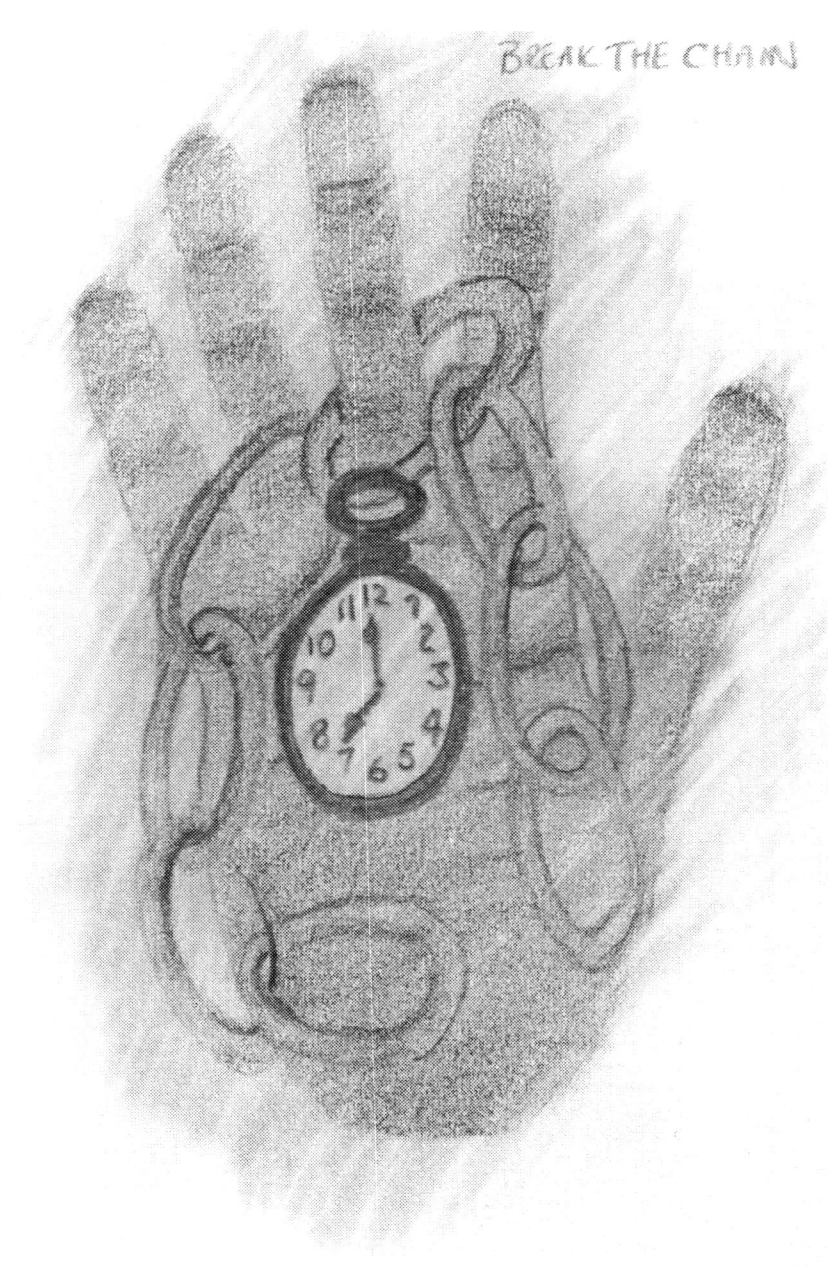

Break The Chain

Will I ever stop feeling this pain?
It's a disease that I pass onto others
Making them feel sadness too.

Will I pass it onto my child as well?
So small and vulnerable
As I was, As I am.

I want to stop it now
Break the chain
This will cause more pain
But, will it be less pain overall?

They say it will
Talking with others, like me
Knowing that I'm not the only one

Take a deep breath in,
The time has come,
To take a chance,
In search of happiness.

STANDING BY

Why do others
Just stand by
And pretend it isn't going on?
Don't they believe?
Can't they believe?
The horrors of this world?

It makes me sick
What he's doing to you
I know how you feel inside
I don't want to remember
It hurts to remember
It makes me wasn't to curl up and die

How do I stop
This getting to me
While still protecting you?

You need to be strong
You need to be brave
You need more help than just me

I'm here for you
I can listen and offer advice
But you're the one to take control

It's your life
Now claim it back
They had no right to take it

It's your future
Your happiness
Now reach out and grab it
And DON'T let go

Just Hanging In

I'm so tired
But scared to sleep
Frightened by my dreams

I ought to eat
Something's stopping me
Inside it blocks my hunger

I need to cry
But the tears won't flow
The pain is just too deep

I look round this room
It's so unreal
Another world I feel I'm in

I want to die
To end this plight
But somehow I'm just hanging in

My Precious Boy

My little boy
How precious you are
I want to give you
   all that I didn't know
I want you to know love
   without a price
I want you to be happy
   and secure
In the love of your Daddy and I

Oh my son
I'm frightened to love you too much
That I might wrap you in cotton wool
Or not let you choose your own path.
I don't want to hold you back
Or push you forward before you're ready
I'm scared that you'll be hurt

I'm your mother
Though I feel so unprepared
I want you to know happiness
To grow, caring and strong

Not knowing the pain I've known
So when you look back on your childhood
You do so with fond memories
Not with sadness and fear
Nor that feeling of having been cheated
Of innocent and happy first years

I Envy You

I suddenly realised
That you really and truly haven't a clue
What I've been talking about,
What I'm going through.

Oh how I envy you
Your naivety.

To have grown up
Knowing your worth
To be loved
To feel loved
To just take it for granted
The way you do.

I'm glad for you
You can't feel my pain
You can't even imagine
What it's like.

And I hope you never can.

The Later Years

Recovering from Depression

Recovering From Depression

Although this started out about recovering from abuse, it's turned out more into recovering from depression. In many ways I have accepted the abuse, I understand now that it wasn't my fault. It was circumstances that led to the conditions whereby abuse could take place. I can look back on it now with the view of an adult who can see that little Janet couldn't have protected herself and had nobody to turn to. Don't get me wrong, those memories still hurt me, but they don't consume me like they once did.

The only time they surface is when the depression hits. People who haven't had depression or another mental illness cannot hope to understand how it feels; as I don't understand what it's like to live with cancer or be blind, because I've not experienced those things. To feel such mental pain that you would believe and I mean truly believe that your children would be better off without you. Then to have to face that you nearly did that to them! Is a hard thing to come to terms with, especially when you're still depressed!

It helps to think of the depression as some sort of parasite, which slips in and controls your mind. But it's also unsettling to know that you're not in control of your own mind. That makes you loose confidence and unable to trust your own judgement. It also effects how others around treat you, even those who accept your mental illness is just that – an illness, will treat you differently.

I am so lucky that I have some of the most amazing friends. They have taken phone calls in the middle of the night; put their plans on hold to be with me because I needed them. Listened while I tried to make sense of what was going on in my head. They genuinely have been there for me.

They've told me this is because I'm also a good friend. I have an insight into others pain; that I'm there for them. With good advise and a listening ear. One insisted that I added this to point out that friendship is two way. I think that one of the most important things about friendship is trust. This is one thing that abuse survivors have a problem with. We don't think that we have the same rights as other people, or that we matter. We've been unable to trust because we've been let down and believed that we were the ones in the wrong. This makes trusting others a leap of faith.

My last depression which I am still in the process of recovering from has shown me that most people are worthy of our trust. Also, you don't have to tell them everything, just to say that you need them, most people will try to be there for you. It is worth making that leap of faith. Maybe if you're not sure about someone, share this book with them and see how they react. I'm pretty sure that the majority of people will agree that it wasn't little Janet's fault. Nor was it yours.

THE WELL

Its dark outside
I can see no light
And the monster lurks up there

Not sure how I find myself
In this deep dark well

Not sure how I fell so far
Into this deep dark well

It's damp and cold
I can hear some sounds
But can't cry out for help

The monster lurks
He'll come for me
I can't cry out for help

How do I escape?
Where do I go?
I can not even move

The monsters here with me
Here inside my head
He tells me what I've got to do
I don't want to, but I must obey
He's trying to take my life away
He's giving me ideas
Subtle is his method
Whispers them, then makes me move

I feel him all around me
He sends tingles round my head
He makes it numb, I can not think
But just follow his commands

This isn't right
It's me not him
It's me that's doing wrong
It's me that's trying to end my days
But why?   I don't understand
It must be me
It can not be
Some other force
But it doesn't make sense
How can I be?
So detached when I do these things

I'm back down
In the cold damp well
Shivers down my spine
My head still spins, so light and free
What's gone on?
I do not know

ABANDONED

Well the pills are working
So off you go

We've bandaged your wounds
You may go home

The pains still there
The pills not so strong
Don't you get it?
THERE'S STILL SOMETHING WRONG!

It was hard enough to ask for help
Now the doors closed in my face

I still need help
All is not well
BUT NOBODIES THERE ANYMORE!

Numb

I cut myself
I'm not sure why
Maybe it's because
I'm numb inside

I seem to switch off
Not sure what's happening
Find myself, somewhere else
In another time

This isn't right
I don't know why
I'm sure there's something
Wrong inside

But they think I'm better
Ready to resume
Get back to life now
On with the struggle

It shouldn't be this way
I don't understand
I keep drifting away
To another land

How do I tell them?
What do I say?
How do I ask for help?
Again, and again, and again

Moving On

Moving on
Away from the pain
The blame, was not mine to take
The past is done
Now, is time, to look on ahead

The future is not pre written
Sadness is not my fate
Time to put away
What's gone before
Time to move on

What awaits me I do not know
But I must leave the past behind
Look forward not back
Otherwise, they've won
But if I look forward
Then my life, will be, My Own.

Silent Scars*

Silent scars
They wait to be seen
Silent scars
Proof of the pain
Where I have been
What I have survived

Silent scars
Deeply embedded
Not just in my flesh
But in my head
The only way to see was fresh blood
To feel that I'm not dead

Silent scars
I need somebody there
Need someone to talk to
Don't push me away don't fear

The silent scars they won't let anyone in
To what's really in my head
Am unable to begin
Silent scars, relief through and through
Just to think I once loved you

Scars are embarrassing
When someone says what's wrong?
Go away leave me alone
I don't want to talk it all feels wrong
Silent scars they hold the past
Silent scars,
They fade but they last.

By Lonely

I Ate Today

Strange that it should be such an achievement
Not sure why?
Why?
Why?
Don't I eat?

Do I want to hurt myself?
Or make somebody notice
That all's not right?

I'm not hungry
But I ought to be
Is my head screwed up?
Stopping me from caring for myself

When I was a child
No one noticed
There wasn't much food anyway
Mother liked to see the pattern on the plate

Now when things aren't right
I seem to revert back,
Back into a little girl

I don't want to be her again
I don't even use her name
So today I ate
And tomorrow I'll eat again!

Morning

I didn't want to face today
Just to stay in bed
Hide from the world
For a little bit longer

Looked out the window
Been raining all night
The flowers are well watered
But I still can't see a reason to rise

So much good, in this world
Got to think positive
Wish I wasn't so tired
Can't believe this is so hard

Be kind to myself
That's what I should do
Be strong and look after myself
Even though I don't want to

How do I find the strength?
To care properly for myself
So much easier to just wallow
In this depression

Winter Returns

It's been like spring
Flowers popped up
Beautiful daffodils
Crocus and Snow Drops
Including me

But the cold is on its way back
Heard it on the weather forecast
Little did they know
They were referring to my story
For relapse is imminent

How do I know?
Went there last night
Been planning it since
Got the pills out
Booze in the cupboard

So the vulnerable little Snow Drop
Is about to be frost bittern
It's so delicate
It won't make it through
Not to the real spring or summer

There's no way back you see
A short release, that's all I got
But back down I was thrown
Need to be taken in from the cold
And nurtured for a while
Maybe then, just maybe
There's a chance I could survive

THE VISIT

I went to visit little me
An Angel told me how

I stood across the road from her
She was at her bedroom window
Looking out so lonesome-ly
I waved to her, she waved me back
A smile across her face
I didn't need to introduce myself
She knew me straight away

Up in her room I found me there
We sat upon her bed
The pale green walls
The stereo, still playing 12th of Never

Off sick from school, Not diagnosed
But I explained what's wrong
They won't know for 15 more years
They don't recognise the signs

I held her close, I held her tight
She cried and I cried too
Why does she feel so all alone?
I tell her, she's got me

I had to leave, I couldn't stay
Back to my world I came
But with me I brought something special
The love from little me

        Thank you Angel Nina; for telling me how to reach her.

Just Thoughts *

He's in my bed
He's in my head
Need to run away
Scared he will find me anyway

He's gone from my bed
But still in my head
Don't need to run away
Still frightened everyday

He can't come to my bed
Pushed to the back of my head
Got to stop running away
Need to get on with my life today

By MoJo

You Matter!

I know you don't think so
I have trouble believing it myself
For years conditioned to believe
That I mattered less than everyone else

Got that wrong!
Been told!
In no uncertain terms!
They were wrong when I was young
I do matter

I matter, just because I am
Just because I'm me

We all touch others
In ways that we never realise

A smile from a stranger, says
"I don't know you, but we're all connected."

So don't try to convince yourself
That you're unworthy in some way
Because if I matter
Then you matter

And if you're feeling down right now
You know you're not thinking straight
Trust me
I've been where you are
And you will come back up,
You Will!
And then you'll be able to help another
Because you'll understand
That they matter too.

Dwelling

Dwelling on thoughts
That I'd rather not think
They keep slipping in
When I'm not expecting

Trying so hard
To fight this depression
To stay strong and affirmative
But I'm getting so tired

Don't believe what I tell myself
Try to tell me I'm worth it
That I'm a good friend
And help others out
But I just don't believe it

The thoughts they slip back in
Creep into my mind
Whisper things to pull me down
Tell me I'm such a drain
So I won't call on others in case they confirm

Niggling doubts about who I am
What is the point of my life?
Where have all my bubbles gone?

AND WILL I EVER GET THEM BACK?

Pull Myself Out

Pull myself out
But how do I pull myself out
What do I hold on to?
What can I reach up for?

Pull myself out
I don't know how to pull myself out
I keep trying to find
The exit from my mind

Pull myself out
Someone tell me how to pull myself out
Where's the key
I still don't know where I am

Pull myself out
Don't feel I can pull myself out
I'm tired, so tired of this fight
Can't the bell ring to end a round?

Pull myself out
Not sure I can pull myself out
So alone, so scared
Just don't feel I can go on

Pull myself out
Put myself out, out of this miserable world
That's the only exit I can see
Surely someone TELL ME WHY?

Pull myself out
I just can't pull myself out
I've nothing to pull on
Please can't someone PUSH ME for a while?

Pull myself out
Out of where, pull myself out of my mind
They say I'm strong
But they're so wrong; I'm all out of pull

Keep Fighting *

When you only cry in the dark
So no one else sees
When you flinch from a flashback
But pretend it's a sneeze

When you smile all the time
Just to make yourself believe
That it might be ok
That you just need to breathe

When you're really a mess
But are too stubborn to call
On anyone for help
As they'll see how you fall

Just keep running my friend
Run faster than lightening
And keep searching and fighting
For a way past this frightening
Mess in your head and numbness in your heart

For one day, I'm certain
Your life will restart

By Sumday

Hold Onto Me

Oh little girl of mine
Thank you for showing me the way
Thank you for being there
For caring for your Mummy

I could only see
Harm that I was doing
I couldn't see how much you needed me
But now it's clear, what I must do
And that is hold on tight to you

You are my strength
You are my goal
For you need me in your world
So I'll be here for you
And we'll see each other through

Together we will win
And you'll show me
The joy I missed
When I too; was a little girl

LET IT BE *

Put it to rest now
Put it to bed
Don't listen to those demons
That run round your head

Flush those pills away now
They don't need to be popped
Put the knives away now
It's time for you to stop

No more throwing up or bingeing
Let it all go, let it be
Give yourself a break now -
For you can, and will, be free

There's no need for you to run now
There's no need for you to fight
Just take a leap of faith now
It's going to be alright.

By Sumday

Resolve

This was meant to happen
Don't know why but it will help
Sometime in the future
I'll be there to understand

The strength I've gained
Through fighting demons
Will guard me for all time

I will come out stronger
Fiercer than before
And Thrive

AFTER THE STORM

There's been a storm
It's all fresh now
The wind and rain have blown away
Those dark and fearsome clouds

This morning I walk
With warmth on my face
See sunshine, peeking through the trees
And wonder what the fuss was about

Giggling children
Barking dogs
Sweet little bird song
Music playing joyfully

Stop and listen
Stop and look
Otherwise you'll
Miss the point

Smell the fragrance
Of pretty little flowers
Feel the breeze
Watch the bees

Don't rush on by
In a great big hurry
It's time to rest
And refresh yourself

Re-charge your batteries
Because more storms will come
But don't forget
What follows them

TRIPPED UP

Ok so I slipped
And I tripped
And fell over again
Got another scar
And some hurt pride

But I knew that I'd stumble
I'm still very weak
And the difference is
I'll just get up
And start to climb again

Each time I fall
I'll pull myself up
Maybe I'll have to rest a while
But up I will get
And start to climb again

And each time I rise
I'll be stronger than the last time
Because I'll know that I've done it before
My muscles will build
As I start to climb again

Then there'll be fewer rocks
And the path will be clearer
With more hand holds to grab onto
There'll be twists and turns
On this long climb up again

But climb I will
For I want to see
The view from up the top
And it will be, glorious to see
For I'll never have been so high before

SQUEEZE MY HEART

My heart beats fast
Pain, nagging in my chest
You're trying to scare me
Grip my heart and squeeze
Because I'm fighting back
Won't let you rule my head
So you're trying another way

I know you want to frighten me
I know your little game
Make me think there's more wrong
But you won't win

You see I've seen this before
All those years
I watched you fight my Mother
SHE GAVE IN
NOT ME

So squeeze my heart
Stab it if you can
Speed up the beats
Yes I feel the pain

But you won't win
Not this mind game!

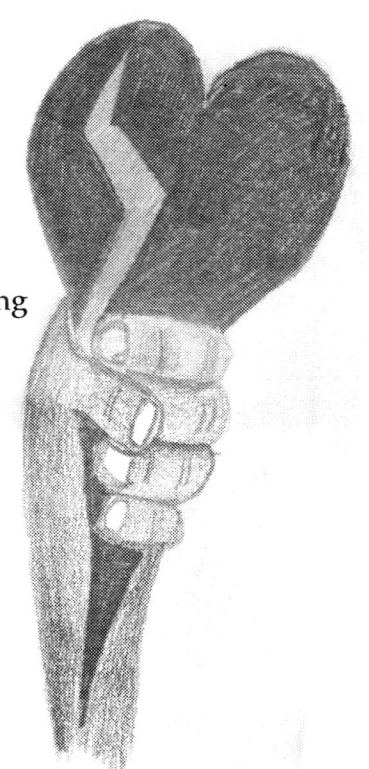

FLOWER

Pretty little flower
Why do you hide for so long?
It's dark and cold down there
And warm and bright up here

Come out
Show yourself
Lets see those gorgeous colours
Smell your sweet perfume

Oh pretty little flower
Why are you so scared of this world?
You had a hard winter
But the spring has come

So pretty little flower
Pop your head up and see
The garden is full of all your friends
Who want to dance & sing with you

You're not meant to hide away
You're here to show your glory
It's OK to be a bit afraid
But you'll soon see, it's safe up here

So rise up
Come on
You can do this
Rise up and enjoy the world

Show You Care

Please don't shed a single tear
Nor, spare me any pity
What's happened, is in the past
I'm in no danger now.

My demons try to trip me up
They invade my dreams
But when I wake, I know I'm safe
And lock them up again

I remember reaching out for help
Eleven I think I was
I tried to explain, but no words came
None that made any sense

Others are in danger
So keep a watch out for them
As they try to ask for help
In their own unusual ways

You can make a difference
You can ease their pain
Just by being there and listening
Showing that you care

For like me, they don't believe
That their worthy of your time
They need to know that they matter
And they will survive, to live a happy life.

Please Yet Again?

Wobbles on the way
Feel them creeping up
I know I'm on the mend
But I'm slipping down again
Not too far I hope
Can someone grab on quick
Reassure me
I can do this
It's all spinning round my head!

Last time
I was on my way back
Screwed up good & proper
Couldn't handle
Facing the crowds
Couldn't face moving on
Got to do this
That I know
But the courage to continue
Is tiring me so

This should be straightforward
I've done it before
But I keep getting dizzy
At just the thought
I want my life back
But this time I want it for me
Not sure how to do that
Never been taught
Mixed up in my thinking

Don't want to ask again
Not sure I'll even send this
Feeling such a drain
But need to get stuff straight
Can't do it on my own
Not sure which bit is wrong?
Don't know how to stop
This happening again

RIDING THE WAVES

Up and down
My little boat goes
Riding the waves of my mind

Up so high
Look up see the sky
See the birds take flight

Deep down low
Sinking fast
Darkness swallows me whole

Trying to steer
Back to safe water
But the storm just keeps on coming

Shout Mayday
Does anyone hear?
Yes, but are they coming?

Got a hole in the hull
Waters are gushing
Tears that just won't stop

Hear voices on radio
Calm and reassuring
Telling me what I must do

Steer straight ahead
Keep the course
The milder weather is coming

Hold on tight
Do not give up
Keep, just keep on going

I'm tired
The waves still lap
And shake my little boat

Blue sky I see
Right up ahead
So steer my boat steadfastly

Keep riding the waves
Determined and single-minded
Stay staunch to the belief, that I will make it

But I'm not sure
Stay stubborn and unyielding
Do not give in, to tricks of the sea

Stay resolute and firm
Be obstinate, it'll see you through
To the beautiful clear water

Snow Drop

The suns coming up
Spring is on its way
The long, cold winter
Soon to hide again

Snow Drop peeping out its head
Is it safe?
Time to bloom?
Buuur bit chilly still

Some kind soul
Nurtures, Warms
Shares their strength
Rise up, show your true beauty

It's time to let go
Let the darkness slip away
Turn the pain into good
Help somebody else on their way

I Claim My Life

It's my life now
No more will the past dictate the future
The pain of that time, gone
It will always sadden me
But it won't ruin my whole life
Those nightmares lift with the sunrise

No more to be afraid
No more to hide
No more to cover up their lies
No more to cry alone
No more will the demons from long ago
Continue to dictate my days

So I plan
To have loads of fun
To do all the things I should have done
Who cares if I'm too old!
I don't
Because it's my life
And I deserve some good times
To make up for all the wrong done

The games I missed out on as a girl
I'll play now with my children
I can skip through fields
Walk along the beech
Run and hide behind trees
Laugh until it hurts
For it's my life now
I CLAIM IT BACK

Where To?

OK it's been hard
The fights not over yet
All that's gone before
Has made me who I am

A friend, to anyone in need
A listening ear, with insight to some horrors
An understanding deeper
Than others who haven't seen

A fighter, strong, resourceful
Who'll battle tooth and nail
Who gets up when she's been knocked down
Who won't accept defeat!

The person you can turn to
When you're in trouble or need help
The person who'll stand by you
Throughout!

TAKE FLIGHT

Like a bird I soar
Watching down
Feel the air beneath my wings
Twisting and turning
Oh the freedom
Oh the joy
Fly high
Fly higher
Up
Up
Then down
But turn
And
RISE AGAIN

Bubbles

Bubbles
I found them
Simmering away
Now they're popping up all around

So happy
Want to play
Lots of things I can do, today
Now my bubbles have been found

Friends

I reached out and you were there
With good advise and a listening ear
I was hurting, pain so excruciating
Didn't want to admit
How deeply I had sunk
Had nothing left to give
Saw no point in carrying on
But I made that leap of faith
And trusted you
You didn't let me down

Took phone calls late at night
Reassured me, it would be alright
Didn't judge me
Argued when I'd got it wrong
Talked when all I could do was cry
Picked me up when I fell down
Encouraged me
Lifted and supported me
You were truly there for me

Thank you my dear friends.

LET ME KNOW

When I first wrote many of these there was no intention of ever publishing. It was just my way of trying to make sense of all the thoughts that whizzed around my head, or my attempts to connect with others, when I didn't know how to reach out to them.

In reading these I have let you into my inner world, many of my poems ask you direct questions. So if you need or would like to respond to anything you've read then please do email me at janet.bale@yahoo.co.uk   I would like to hear from you and will try to reply to all emails.

There are also many groups who exist to help, such as EVA Emerging from Violence & Abuse a Women's Aid Charity (www.rcwa.org.uk); profits from the sale of this book are supporting their work so that they can continue to be there for survivors of abuse.

I also recommend www.angelsurvive.com you may meet me there, my nickname is Snow Drop.

I don't know if I ever will fully come to terms with my past; but I do know that I have done good things with my life. What happened shaped who I am today; but it does not need to be a shadow across my future, I am now happy, and know that I actually do matter. I matter to my children and to my friends, I make a difference to others and most importantly I now matter to me!